al Festival Hall

Claude Vigée

Flow Tide: selected poetry and prose

edited and translated by Anthony Rudolf

additional translations by: Willis Barnstone, Keith Bosley,
Cid Corman, W.S. Graham, Jonathan Griffin, J.R. LeMaster
and Kenneth I. Beaudoin, Patricia Terry

Menard/King's
London
1992

Flow Tide: poems and prose by Claude Vigée
© 1992 Éditions Flammarion or the author (see note on p9 for details)

Translations © 1992 Anthony Rudolf or the other translators

The Menard Press/King's College London wish to thank Claude Vigée and Éditions Flammarion for their co-operation.

Acknowledgements: some of Anthony Rudolf's translations have appeared in Ariel, Cambridge Review, Jewish Chronicle, Jewish Quarterly, Middle East Co-existence, Shirim, Tel-Aviv Review, in the book Decadel (Sceptre Press 1979) and the anthology Voices in the Ark (Avon Books, New York, 1980).
Willis Barnstone's translation appeared in Modern European Poetry (Bantam Books, New York 1966).
Cid Corman's translation appeared in Origin XI, 1953.
W.S. Graham's co-translation with Vigée appeared in Heritage 1, vol 2, 1949.
Jonathan Griffin's translations appeared in the proceedings of the European Poetry Festival, Leuven.
Our thanks to all the editors for publishing the translations (sometimes in earlier versions) in the first place.
Thanks to Freema Gottlieb © 1992 for permission to edit extracts from her interview with Claude Vigée. An earlier version appeared in The Jewish Chronicle.

Cover design by Merlin James

Distribution in North America by SPD Inc
1814 San Pablo Avenue
Berkeley, CA 94702, USA

ISBN 0 9513753 7 7

The Menard Press   King's College London
8 The Oaks   Adam Archive Publications
Woodside Avenue   Strand,
London N12 8AR   London WC2R 2LS
081 446 5571

Typeset by Wendy Pank
Book production by Fakenham Photosetting Limited
Printed by The Iceni Press

CONTENTS
(all translations by Anthony Rudolf, unless otherwise stated)

5

NOTE

All the poems up to 1972 have been collected in *Le Soleil sous la mer*, Flammarion 1972. *Délivrance du souffle* (1977), *Pâque de la parole* (1983), *Feu d'une nuit d'hiver* (1989), from which later poems have been selected, are all published by Flammarion. *Apprendre la nuit* (1991) is published by Arfuyen. The four new poems are, as yet, unpublished in the original.

Prose: *Journal de l'été indien* was published by Gallimard in 1957. The other three books, as listed in the contents, are all published by Flammarion.

The introduction is to appear in *Dans le silence de l'Aleph*, Albin Michel 1992.

Freema Gottlieb recorded her full conversation with Claude Vigée at his apartment in Paris early in 1991.

INTRODUCTION

We experience a good and a bad silence. The good silence involves listening, opening the soul to art, to light and to darkness, to the initial utterance from which all the others could emerge in the course of a life. King David, in psalm 40, thanks God for having so deeply "hollowed out his ear". Withdrawn into us, hidden behind a veil of forms, of images, of fugitive events, the place of total trust and plenitude shelters peacefully – sometime I call it the lake of dew – from which flows, out of silence, the possibility of perception of things, and at the same time, the possibility of speech.

Of course, the material, physical, biological and historical conditions of our life often stand athwart the road which leads to this utopian dwelling place. The obstacles of daily life present a thousand traps on the path of this original bursting forth. We endure, we breathe, we speak, we survive from moment to moment by virtue of this sacred place hidden within ourselves, by the gift of its quickening dew; and against the adversaries who bar our way, forbid us access, sometimes for long years...

We are engaged at every moment in this incredible struggle with the angel. The sooner we realise the conflictual nature of our banal everyday trials, the better it will be for us. Little by little we will become conscious of the simultaneity of those two opposed energies: the force of uplift and the impulse of arrest – the stranglehold of the brake, the weight of radical dejection. For we are the terrain of this endless battle.

But above all and after all, a power of indomitable emergence fortunately asserts itself, a place of total trust, whose metaphor is silence. In every meaning of the word, silence as speech incapacity, refusal to speak, injunction to be silent, deep-seated difficulty in living, and also the good silence, the silence of disinterested listening to the Other – all silence proceeds from that place where the lake of inner dew sparkles: it is the place within us of primal unity. But it involves active simplicity, a mute and effervescent presence like that of the letter Aleph (the One) in the Hebrew alphabet.

That listening, which demands silence, the forgetting of all instrumental use of language, provisional renunciation of the power of the word, is the way towards this place. Listening without making, without the various means of replying, a listening without images – initially deprived of fantasy, or personal memories – the listening which is at the same time a laying bare, allows us access in flashes to the happy and terrible place of full trust. It is not really the site of our birth, for it precedes our arrival in this world, it is upstream of every birth.

Births and battles, every struggle, every exile, every return are its fruits, ripened on the tree of life planted in its silt, at the very heart of that Eden lost since its non-existent origins. "For nothingness (Ayin), which is blessed wisdom, is the course of life, of well-being and of pleasure. It is the Eden which transcends the future world" (Book of Tanya, IV, ch.8).

My experience of war, of exile, of America, taught me from my early youth to thirst for this place. Circumstances compelled me to dig myself an underground tunnel towards it. Then came the return. This journeying out of historical time seemed to me more rigorous than biographical exile. Its demands are even harsher than the obstacles one must confront throughout a long life. The journey towards the green source of evening silence, towards the secret realm of the Aleph, contains at the same time the promise of a reversal, of a turning from the past towards the unheard-of future, as well as a free opening to the world. Not only a decisive opening to the universe of sensations, but also initiation into the world of speech, forbidden right from the start.

This silent listening is linked to our experience as young Alsatians born just after the first world war: we were condemned by European destiny to an artful speechlessness of metaphysical dimensions. It prepared me for the exploration of mute inwardness, brusquely laid bare, which leads on occasion to discovery of the primal space: the inaudible kingdom of Aleph buried within oneself.

Not to have a language of education approved by the monster of social and scholarly conventions, to feel from earliest childhood the stern interdict placed on our mother tongue, that dialect excluded from the realm of good by the caprices of continental history in the first quarter of the twentieth century: these are ideal conditions for the rending which drove us to an ominous withdrawal, a radical and inner exile – into that absolute place which is not yet myself, but the living spring which shall be – elsewhere and beyond – the radiant dark centre of all my selves. Situated there, is a fundamental I of which the self belonging to each of us, mine among them, constitutes a multiple flowering, across the time of this world dragging us towards the abyss.

The point of departure was in the withdrawal towards the vacant and nameless place of full trust, and in the reverse movement which, starting with the nucleus of the initial pulsating fire, permits us to flow, to leap towards an undefined future life. Above all take care not to describe it, not to spell out its limits. Once there, know how to dance to the end; dance within speech, and dance in the body beyond our everyday space, with others who allows themselves to be caught up in the rhythmic motion. Only there can one truly encounter other people – on the same track as yourself...

If my poems, my narratives, my testimonies, are going to serve any purpose, is it not to clear a path towards the place of that primal trust? And then like a drill to thrust throught to the other road, reverse but parallel – a twin brother of the first: opening to the inhabited time and space of this world, wherein we plunge as a river flows towards the ocean, pouring out as it goes the seed of its great waters sparkling in the rising evening, freely fecundating the belly of the earth.

Claude Vigée, 1992

POETRY

EASTER SONG

I drifted to a distant land
There was no time or place:
I only heard the cry of barren cities.
Atlantic, well of blood choking the heart,
In your stone vise between dry fear and dawn
We cannot wrest from the dark hive of sleep
Our song lost in labyrinths of shrieks.
But one star crowned with thorns and scars
Bleeds on debris of all our continents.
When fire flares from this nightswollen corpse
Keys fall from the sky to the wrists of the sea;
Thawing trees crash down upon our heads,
A thousand birds dazed from kindling night
Which dance towards death beneath a sun of
        thunder.
In their divided wood a caskful of cold
And flaming ermine wreathed in diamonds
Drunk at heavy wells breaks up in silence.
Notching upon the roofs their velvet knives
Midnight lightnings are thrust into walls
And windows burnt by lips of storm
Breathe in the ardent swell of spring.
But one head crowned with thorns and scars
Radiates this dawn on all our continents.
Borne to eclipse between ice and light
The birds of thaw have blinded our lids.
We dance for the dead in the wind's orchard.

(With one great breath I launch their name on
        future air
Like algae opening on the seas.)

17

WESTERN ISLE

Arrow of frozen blood, aerial grenade...!
Under the willows' claws
twisted in a fire of heather
whirls a bird around the devastation
of a pond covered with black rime.

Praise in a secret cry!
She-wolf, dead or alive, in the heart's icy well?
Lightning flash: thin squirrel
on the stumps of thunder,
in what paths woven with the panes of spiders,
with roots of salt, burned ivy: winter,
through what dead childhood at the woods' deep
      core?

Flame in the fir-trees.
                    Knives on the vines.
Diamantine clumps. Birds like a sword.
Morning's daughters snatched up by the snow,
Skates' ellipses on the broken ice.

On whom fell your grapnel, mirror of snow-clad
      women,
brand of an eye without silvering, octopus of
      afflicted women,
sun of the extinguished heart?

The crows were gleaming in the midnight sun
but the she-wolf was howling slowly in the well.
On her slate tongue between the frosty gums,

some grains of maize like otters' teeth.
In the snow our blue-gloved dogs swooped down
on her heart-rending eye the sun can't kill.
Flights of feathers burst forth from her slit throat.
A bird's cry burns in her bare nostrils
and cuts out rocks of wind from the light!

The trees of sleep light up again in you
when their white tumour obliterates the sky.
O well of blood glazed with dazzling ice,
you know the rubies of silence,
the axes of purity.

April twilight in New England,
roofs flowing from the sky's groove
weep soot
and a thaw.

Flowering thorn bushes taper across the sea.

But nothing, save the thirst of rivers for autumn ,
announces the wine harvest to the abandoned
        heart
and the bird ablaze in full flight
silent sheds its leaves
in the forest of the ground
till the hour for plundering the funeral coombs –

Exile, o difference,
winter of the word,
heart of nothing beating for night

across the wilderness
of our years,

you glow
like a silence,

love's cold rose
flowering

for the winter
of the heart

WAITING CIRCLE

A sky of blood
scored with cold blue swords
moves over your heads.
Take care, you who weren't engendered
by exile: today
you shall lose your native land,
and into the endless journey towards
solitude,
you'll take with you only your childhood.

Those who made complaints while they were happy
and could not figure what was wrong with me,

and all those who believe I speak in riddles
because they sense the dawning of enlightenment
will understand me in a flash and they will know
the truth: that I am but their own death struggle.

EARTH WITHOUT MEN

About five p.m. upon leaving school
the children go coasting on the white hill

Aiming in the embrasure a finger of dead bark
the fine fretting of cedar boughs
between the simple house and the icy knolls
broods untiringly at the cracked pane
where the wrist of the nightwoodsman bleeds

The stiff grass waits under the frozen pools
Shall we with our eyes of salt ever dare
to face the unicorn at the fountain's heart?
Heat will rush up only through the hidden spring:

To steep our bodies in the live almond bath
we must forget whatever is interposed
we must abandon the ineffectual word
and go down with empty hands to the stream
where the crescent of knowing incurvates

Dawn resplendent on the evening turf
open to us the orchard of your natal womb
We die of cold within the winter of this world
let us glean some fruit from childhood's vines

No longer can we endure interminable hoping
no longer do we need an unheard-of tongue
across the many winters snowing in our mouths
we hear from afar the call of creatures

A mine blast redeems us from the shafts of exile
earth and sky celebrate their nuptials in the wind
the great willow suckled by human sap
springs with summer out of hidden sources

Green mists of forests and cross-poled fields of hops
about five p.m. upon leaving school
in the dampness of June the boys and girls
come blackberry picking at the foot of chestnuts
as a swarm of hornets rise from under the firs
into the mute surging of the light

The children go coasting on the white hill
O Schneewelt der Kindheit
darfst du noch schweigend singen?
by dint of silence by dint of distance
our throat is choked and can sing no more
our love is worn away
by dint of voyages
memory's gone
we're left without speech

In bonnets of fur and scarlet jackets
the boys go coasting on the slope in the wind
flat on their sleds quicksilvered runners
they plunge to the sea the icy traces burst

Against the air the birches rub their ashen backs
pulling their manes on the thorns of the sky
they run into space and kick to the light
a star has flowered within their highest branches

The children have all died
on the white hill

For Jorge Guillén
from one Moon to the other

KINGDOM OF ASHES

On feast-day evenings birches silently
Explode, connected to the ocean tables.
Their lean greyhounds are braced upon the snow:
They set the coal-rich body of lagoons
On fire, stretched out beneath the tall black scrub.

A wind as grey as shale rears from the sea
And cuts the crystals singing in the dunes.
The knives of winter hum about the stumps,
Night-flying gulls flash out across the sky.

Some iron barrels weathered by the sand
Are slowly sucked into the frozen slime
Deep in this ground, this workers' suburb where
Eight children play all Sunday with a ball
Between old newspaper shredded by rats.

O live fish-spawn, O jellyfish of fog,
On your high meadows with their gills of light
We gulp night's concentrated spring: O drop
The snow upon us of your solitude!

As birds of passage feel the rush of air,
We push through exile's timeless space towards
A world where blindness takes the place of night.

A flight of eagles swirls on the Dead Sea,
The moon plays the dark circle of their claws,
Their ram-like faces and their ashen eyes.

My people, all the foreign rivers past,
Are back among the orange groves at last.
We shall not leave these glassy forests now.

VIGIL OF SILENCE

You gulls that wheel down to the shore of exile,
Your wings have dazzled us throughout the night!

The moon was glittering in the spate of tombs,
We made for home, our hair weighed down with
       snow;
Our fingers gripped the flower and the pine cone
Where love and death combine their sombre fires.

You dog, chilled on the rocks when the ice melts,
You sniff the thaw, the scent of it in woods:
Is it the poison of earth, rising again
From the Rhine forest this September when
The meadow-saffron sun distils its bane?

Moulding their velvet steps in snow,
Cats slipped between the hedges,
Cocks burned there in January.

As the sunflower upon the bricks of evening
Wraps its seed-disc in lightnings, man is born
Speechless and all things after are made flesh.

Given to all things, from all things detached,
Being ourselves is useless in this world:
We must learn loss of self, how to be dumb,
Commit our face of foam and sand to none
But the wind dancing at the tempest's tip.
Upended oak, lapping the sap of stars,

27

The hoarfrost crackles, trickles through your
        leaves:
Gaps in your bark are bleeding arteries
Where it will enter you, and there abide.

FLASH OF PRESENCE

In the mountains of Safed, to fan their thirst,
the kings of splendour would bathe in the snow.
Ari – sun's lion –
where are you hiding, morning's gloomy archangel?

Exile of the word, exile of presence;
when the prince is absent
the world itself is in exile
every man is exiled in time's desert.

Shall we know how to free
from the hell of confinements
the light mislaid from wrecked ships?
Under the pyre of Isaac offered up
to the wounded God,
already the ram is crying in the thicket of thorns,
redemption's horn sounds through the flames.

BALANCE SHEET OF HISTORY

Carriers of memory,
messengers without message.
Then this child was born:
the river found a face.

We no longer care
about history's flow:
blood's is enough:
life is now.

I drink the sun
I hold your breast
in my naked hand.

All that is not
finger in the wound
remains unknown to me.

BIRTH OF THE WORLD

Blue and yellow flowers cover the ground of the
      forest,
beneath the pines a sea of ferns is choppy,
in its furrow of granite the raspberry-cane flower
      wakes up.

My daughter runs among the wind-coloured
      butterflies
spotted with aquamarine and shooting stars:
a spike of grass sings as it brushes against her
      naked back.

Her small shoulders sparkle with foam
as she plunges laughing into the torrents of the
      Vosges
in her green and white check costume.

We are all saved.

NUPTIALS

We passed each other
briefly in the night,

but were lost again
in the wind the rain.

Since you revealed
love's forest to me

my tree put down roots
in your naked springs,

and our hands over-
whelmed by the blazing

storm no longer know
which trunks embrace each

other in their night.

FERRYMAN OF STARS

If you feel a river with living waters flowing
        through yourself
outline in your palm
a mirror to contain their inner planets.

Set your kingdom ablaze
in the blood's fire it reflects,
and let its secret plants of summer flower.

But let the lightning filter
only between the rare eyelashes
worthy of sustaining the fire which consumes them.

Plunge through the rocks to bless
in them your nakedness:
thus night

opens on unending stars,
on beaches and birds,
on forests and on winds.

In his boat, heading for human lands,
his seaweed arms
nailed to the masts of memory,
the poet is ferryman
of the fire of origin.

YOU SPEAK TO BE

No more do you
write to be
read by poets.

You speak,
simply,
to enter into
the hearts of men.

Your song is like
a window
open to the wind:

Storm
with a thousand heads.

WIND'S PLACE

The trees born
in this year of life,
the fruit ripening
in this year of life,

the men who died
in this year of life,
and the winter cider
in this year of life,

drunk straight out of
the jug late one night,

show you the knot
of embers in the wind,
where heart and night
are reconciled.

SUN OF DEPTHS

Roses, for the moment,
roll from the heavens:
the world then wakes up
more beautiful than the sun.

The air becomes so clear
that it covers the earth again
in a cloud surpassing
the brightness of a splendid ghost.

High places are filled
only with scenes of us:
when my eye returns

to lose itself in the asphalt
sometimes your face
is exalted in a star.

WORLD'S GAZE

Blue pines
and grey pigeons.
Rocks.
Snow.
Cloud.

You discover your life
in what you give.
Your own death watches you
in what you take.

Blue pines
and grey pigeons
Rocks,
Snow –
Faces.

WINTER

You must have been cold
        to incarnate winter,
without growing pale
        to ice-coat a cedar

which in the night bends
        its white skeleton
under the last star
        dropped in the sea.

If your heart hates the cold,
        become ice-like yourself:
change yourself in spirit
        into its inhuman snow.

Your transformation
        can redeem a universe;
a thousand dawns will flower
        on your winter tree.

Through metamorphosis
        the agony will end:
summer will come again
        out of your coldness.

DESTINY OF THE POET

It is always someone else,
The silent You speaking to himself in me.
Sometimes I tear myself away from the listening
      that is prayer

And I sing in his name in a language borrowed
From the mouths of the dead. For him in me, for him,
Who is already translating me
Into other men's throats.

THE PHOENIX OF MOZART

Arisen from what childhood
the bird of origins? In darkest hell
it sings with the adorable
mouth of an angel.

And this voice alone can save us from silence,
though we wanted to follow it
and shall die with it

and hear nothing
but our cries in the night,
when the rings of the wind on our upturned wrists
revolve their strange fires.

THE WITNESS

At the end of the grey garden
lit up by three birches,
in the cave where I write
in New England,

the sun sets only
through the entrance.
Poet buried
in my stone lamp,

I shut out the light:
with space abolished
the eye tells the exact day,

and the heart does not forget
if it maintains contact
with the gold of the earth.

NUNC DIMITTIS

Walled up in the ghettos
Of history, God said:
"I speak aloud at night
To hush up silence".
Across so many echoes
No executioner heard
The voice of Presence.
On the day of judgment
God himself then came,
Did violence to them,
Crying on their flesh-heaps:
"Victim, in you I am loved".
Blood always unites
The wound and the blade.

NOCTURNE
(Cambridge, Mass)

I am carried far off by a wave of strangers
running through identical and nameless streets
along a brick wall where red and green neon
signs make a hole in the naked sky.

Under the iron moon in the gutter the wind
disembowels a ragged pile of old papers.
A piece of ice cracks
under whose heel, striking the black pavement?

Caught in the shoals of an ebbing life
I drift ever further from the lost house
towards winter where each day we die a little more:
I enter *my* home where solitude is shining.

APRIL

I am born of turbid blood:
My nature is double.

Kittens of the birch trees
rain through my green night.

On trunks sundered
by the frosted moon,

my solar pollen laughs:
stars, wind and sand.

Mother-water fills my valleys:
O uterine blackness.

But the foamy thickets,
green gold on my summits....

Doves and genistas,
ride my whirlwind!

WORLD'S WORD

Brother, I am no stranger:
                    each poem is inscribed
in the night of exile, under a lonely sky,
with memories which bleed without a cry.

Today, bitter honey of a life,
I give back to you these simple words,
learned when I was studying before the war:

mingled with a strange land, with the light,
and darkened in the dying autumn wood,
across the country of an endless wait
they were lost, like me, until the morning.

But the world is blazing in my heart's song,
brother of little faith dying in your house.

EVERY LAND IS EXILE

Every land is exile,
Every language foreign,
After so many turnings, after so much useless
    wandering,
And rich only with oblivion, Oh my
    bitter childhood,
There you are, returned to the poisoned river
Where you drank ruin with the troubled water of
    births.
Lean over its mirror: face of the absent one,
Every word is flight and rootless leaf,
Every bird, sky's prey, bereft of origins.

THE FOREST IS RESTLESS

The forest is restless
At the end of your arms:
You must move fast
To climb over there
On those high branches
Which cast their white
Flowers to the wind
For a short time.
Be quick my spirit,
Climb on the ridge
Then die in the sun:
Awakening's moment
Alone is what counts.

OVER THERE IN ANGUISH

Over there in anguish, but here for joy,
we begin our vigil among the hills;
wandering over the hills
we await the dawn,
with songs and dances in the vines of winter.
There is a great joy in this people:
the joy of return,
brightness of the land where presence shines
from the sky's dark waters
down to the wells in the stone.
Only wanting is the fire
in men's hands.

WITHOUT MEASURING THE TIME

Without measuring the time
of the oil in the lamp,
every mortal flame
flows even hotter, and even higher
is consumed. The lightning flash
crashes down to destroy the rock:
flame's return – at last the face
which so long
shone for night's sake
is scorched!
Shortest-lived place
meeting-point at the extreme,
autumn's bed
where an eternal feast shall die,
time of touching fingers, shaking knees,
cry of fainting bodies the only flame
– where all visible being is exalted
to the very ashes – twists around.

CELEBRATE WHAT WORLD

Celebrate what world, language of our loss?
Clothe what triumph in the purple of ruins?
High in the cold the linen of the clouds
Flaps above the house in the winter storm.
Jerusalem wind, you run across the mountain
Like the rumble of the day about to be.
We had little joy; and yet a festive
dawn is upon the earth.

RETURNING FROM TEL-AVIV

Returning from Tel-Aviv, in the night coach...

Empty grottos of the evening, by the sea. Fog, streets
wandering amid the debris. Jaffa. Ruins in the
distance.

And, once again, that cry emerges from the sea...

Cold black sand. Frozen, radiant turbulence of the
song.

With children grown up, you become living water
once again for there is nothing, but nothing, which
can prevent you from dying.

Returning from Tel-Aviv in the night coach, on the
road strewn with crushed jackals.

EVIDENCE

Evidence:
    Daylight.
Evy, dance!
    Delight.

POETRY

What then is poetry?
A camp fire, abandoned,
smouldering on
the deserted mountain
throughout the night
in summer.

WITHDRAWAL FROM THE WORLD

Withdrawal from the world and from myself,

from the mountain's rubble
I have often heard it spring:
the silent rumble
where thunder will be born.

POET'S LAW

Better than the great idea,
more than the impure image,
rhythm alone is king:
storm or woman's hair,

I hear the beating
of the world's blood
through the acute
ear-drums of rain,

like a torrent
filled with dark light
rolling its icy gold
towards the deep black
ear of earth:

chasing towards
the opening of
an artery's thin bed
the flash of a sword
snatched
from night's rusty lungs.

SALT FLAKES

Distant words, forbidden like your things,
And mingled in the world with ancient mornings,
Slowly, in the night, I move towards you.

Speech relives itself on lips as sealed
As those of the walls which close up the Dead Sea:
Flakes of salt hewn in the heart's deep mines.

EVERYONE IS BORN FROM LOSS

Everyone is born from loss. The immigrant
pitches his tent on the beach.
Wave after wave – stranded in the lilies.
Who can help, who save
the man in league with the outside world?
Come back to the bare place. The father's seed
ripens in the mortal brightness of the earth.

OUR CHILDREN HAVE BUILT...

Out children have built their nest in the fig-tree,
they live among its leaves which hum with light.
World, round and fragile, of bending branches.
Above the tiles on fire, near the low wall without
        gates,
swaddled with jute and golden straw,
the fig tree shall increase in the future place:
out of the sand has risen a town by the sea.

HEAT ON THE WALL

Heat on the wall:
wine harvest thick and cloudy.
Houses crushed by the millstone of the sun
tumble in the sand
among the cries of children.
Sheltered by a vine, the kitten sucks
and rubs its mother's belly with silent paws.
The green lime held out
by the tree over the stone
darkens in the sun.
Black is the weight of the world.

CHALLENGE TO THE NIGHT

I blew the horn of memory this evening
And all those lying down inside their silence
Rose to the summons of that melody.

The crystal trees arisen from my shadows
Break – spinning like a star of fire –
The opaque wall where absolute death rains down.

By the waters of childhood,
The spiritual reef
Where man tamed the angel:
This place is Phanuel
The ford of birth.

You shall go no further, death, for here begins
The land of love that sprang up in my words:
The hand of the infant drinking milk awakens
Like flesh's flower opening in the night,

As excess of pleasure stiffens his two thumbs
He wails sweetly after every mouthful;
His eyes are half-closed in his tiny bald
Head, reflecting freshly broken slate.

He sleeps, drinks: one fist clenched, the other one
        half-open:
The lines of his hand sink deep into the silk:
The rounded cradle smells of curdling milk,
Is filled with the heat of his fat nape.

Outside, the dark world rustles in the mist,
The flowering orchards overflow with silence –
You shall go no further, death, for here begins
Dawn's fable, and here does end the story.
This place is Phanuel, the ford of birth.

Defended by love, by song, by light, man joins
Eternal rear-guard battles with time: against
The patient invasion of the night, a child
And a poem are our tokens of life.

SONG OF OCCIDENT

Song of occident:
Death grinding its grain.
Till the last moment
Re-sifting its refrain
The cracked disc goes round
With a creaking sound.

THE WANDERER

Thin feet are caught
In the grey stones,
Walk here and there,
Anywhere, nowhere,
Stumbling under autumnal stars.

The heart is in the middle,
It does not fix in rocks, in words,
It is not lost on this side of the world
In the sombre silence of the void.
Beneath this humid garden
Abandoned at night
Among the dark rose-trees,
The earth itself, abandoned, shines.

Indeed it's worth the trouble
Of returning to the world,
Bearing its fruit,
With tears and hard work,
With no hope but the shadow,
Without watching for daylight.

MY TONGUE IS THE BLADE...

My tongue is the blade
which frees the stele.
On my open lips
lodges a glow-worm:
fire hidden
between my teeth,
I am sawing
the still opaque
face of presence
– I, the servant
of an irrepressible
arousal:
a black stallion
from the depths of childhood
announces within me
a measureless neigh,
accomplice of joy
arriving earlier
than its countenance.
My breath carves it
a delicate face
the colour
of ripe clay
lit by a rainbow.
But black indeed
        grace appeared
            in the beginning.

INSIDE THE CAMP OF JUDAH...

Inside the camp of Judah
in the midnight market
Yemenite youths
their eyes dark as wells
carry with great care
their baskets over-
flowing with fruit.
Announced in the sky
by the solemn plainsong of crickets
the procession moves forward
ceremonious beneath the wind
which falls from adoring stars.
The world embalms the gourds
melons and apricots.
The abandoned shops
cradle in the shadows
their heavy sacks of spice
filling the glowing space
with invisible tiles.
Behind the conniving gates
folded back to earth
fornicates
a wild she-cat
rattling in the night
like the Shulamite
for she is mad with love.

TO BE BORN...

To be born
       fall
            breathless
in between the narrow
thighs of night our mother

Then to whirl
           gasping
down time's black marble spiral
staircase
         as far as
the second strait: dismemoried infinity.
Below, the desert river flows, imperceptible
sewer:
         oval mouth of the labyrinth – a deafening
pipe which debouches
into the sea where every gleam of voices is dowsed.

First you die of life
Then you live off murder.
That happens unaided
without giving us trouble.
Evening
         at the telly
while the children sleep

death faithful actor
is always in the programme
Very early. Much too late.

OUT OF EXILE...

Out of exile
I climbed up to this place,
not to keep
silent in the fire
nor to sleep
as a God
in the ancient sepulchre
of a shady, indestructible
and bloodless dream,
but to find
my tongue there
and enjoy myself, and live
as every poet lives: a stranger
among my own.

After the cold, the darkness
of a world without
speech, hatching peril,
here I am
new, facing
the morning of the virile
olive-tree
grown old in the danger
of the time
of endless daily war,
speaking as a free man,
joyous and comforted
by my burden of hope.

Dancer with bloody feet

already surging,
I bring tomorrow into
the world, simply
by my presence,
announcing a happiness
beyond farewells.

WITH MY OLD NET

With my old net
      repaired, full of holes,
made of torn words,
      tears and laughter,
slowly I drew
      a basket heavy with life
– like a foundling –
      out of the Nile of oblivion

FLOW-TIDE

In the nameless land of absence without end
I flow back after you, my faceless shadow;
when the rain thrums at the decline of summer
on the parched earth
nothing now lights up the unconquerable dusk:
no warmth from above melts
the opaque ice of the soil,
no dawn breaks on the heart of the abyss;
nothing brightens or reconciles
agony's mere horror.
The heavy and ripe moon sheltered in clouds
flees like a sand-heap in the alley's black depth;
only the wind returning builds its holy house.
Autumn's incense offered in scent of sadness
strains to reach the night on the year's far bank.

It's still the good-bye hour in this valley of shadow:
heart's exhaustion, the too long-drawn-out circling
towards the agony where a sunless morning burns
always further from you, deserted childhood,
you my sweet, my inconsolable bitterness!
Across the forest, upstream of sleep,
I return to the garden: fires of branches smoulder
against the ruined wall – black and green hearth –
below the deserted house where winter homed,
As far as the forbidden place: near the first belly.

To be there
in
        the crumbling of the stones

                    expecting
what, nothing?
the wind falling heavy and weary
on the aged eye-lids:
death is the dreamer of the dream of my life.
Who will tell you secret, under the brambles of
        hoar-frost,
childhood's narrow empty and black boat
forgotten on the pool, at the end of November,
in the white funerary forest of Ried?

THE FIRE OF A WINTER NIGHT

When the evening sun freezes in the fir-cone
like an icicle hung on the highest branch
at the wood's edge, behind Hare Leap,
turn again into the sinking day's light
and cast a long look, for the last time,
at your desire dying in the trees in flames:
anguish of enjoying, horror of the gape
nourish in turns the poet's dream.
Look at them passing in the distance, in reverse
        order;
when you see them thus filing in silence
by the other end of your opera-glasses,
they all are signalling to you goodbye:
for already, over your life, slowly night falls.

In the same seed-corn
your hidden seasons
grow to one another.
Yet the germ sleeps and dreams
beyond thoughts;
into the dark subsoil it plunges
where abruptly opens
a child's face
with which the grain rises
between the straw towards the sky,
out of the brown earth
to lips torn by the winter plough-share.

To some, profusion is given for ever
from the beginning:

but to whom? and why?
So powerful a miracle
is not the simple fruit
of a germ, merely:
in it is incarnate also
the work of clement weather,
the black oblation of the land,
the unnamed effort of the peasant.
For every creature there comes one rare instant
propitious to the flaming of maturity.
Each of us writes only a quite small chapter
in the log-book of the terrible voyage.

Pity quivers at the heart of the invisible star
that brings forth the world out of the dark almond.
When the evening sun, dying of solitude,
freezes with the last fruit of the heavenly fir-tree
at the foot of Hare Leap, on the border of the woods,
the village crumbles suddenly into night:
a ship in distress, heavier than lead,
slowly gets low in the water, then abruptly founders
without a cry into the sombre deep of the sea.

Within it, men keep passing each other close,
groping in the dark, the way blind men do:
each one becomes for the other a sightless limit,
a shadow that slides escaping near the walls
about the narrow soaked suburban alley
where the rain goes on pouring and rolls in a torrent
from the slate roofs sloping to their grey gutters,
to spout again, lower, in great empty yards!
A well, spread out wide like some hollow orbit,

gapes abroad at the cloudy Christmas sky.
It's waiting for, at midnight, the frozen eye of the
    moon
running on high among December's storms
– down through the chimney's hole
to the bottom of the factory in ruins
darting its fixed stare, dazzled with whiteness –
to dilate dreaming over the foreign land.

FUTURE AIR

Goat offered up at new moon,
I murmured over the water
the unutterable name.
Already in my vertebrae
the blind serpent
awakens.

The darkening glow
of a fire of dead branches
in the empty forest
at the end of autumn
answers the setting sun
trapped in the hard frost
that the black pond
bristling with scrub erodes –

deep in twilight where the sly
fog glides patiently:
grey serpent
of silence

THE HOPE OF THE TWELFTH HOUR

"I will wait daily for his coming"

Black motionless sun
At the zenith of my night,

A lone crow leans over
The finger of the cypress:

The bird mounts guard at
The gates of the secret.

Prisoner of roots,
Time never ceases

Breaking its light
On the tablets of stone.

Silence, unique is child of my cry!

And though he tarry
I will wait

Until the raid of my last dawn,
Mournful sun ripening in my darkness.

THE SURFACE OF THINGS

I
Behind the rusty grating of the ruined asylum
they sowed green grass
in black mud over us.

In the December wind
the grass now is dry and hard:
beneath the hoarfrost some grey dust endures,

in the cold and shattering brightness of the
        wasteland.

II
They sowed green
grass and black
dust over us

The green grass now is ash
in the inert light of evening.

Of it and of us will remain
only fallow – extinguished

beneath the sad and dirty mildew of the snow.

HOME IS THE SECRET

Home is the secret
whose exile was quest:
wandering presence
in the desert wind.

We shall return
to the lost house
thanks to hushed words,
overcome by silence.
Lips always moving,
cuts and ties, passage
of the living, hiatus
crossed in one go
between letter and breath:
the secret of home
is rooted in a cry,
its silence my source.

In memory's void
the one word springs up
reviving its light,
like the flame of
the candle keeping
watch in the darkened
room of the dead.
Word out of silence,
born from the memory
of nothing, engendered
out of the void, brought
forth in the shelter

of remembrance and
of oblivion.

Amid the mortal
here, we shall find
our ultimate recourse
elsewhere, we possess
a no-place of return
elsewhere, a good-place
elsewhere, a faith kept
in the welcoming
elsewhere, over there
where the evening
light, green, dies
and flowers again
over the silent spring!

In the betrayed
place of listening
exile renewed
takes root. The safety
vault closes again
on the undeserved treasure.
But the lost land
remains ours in secret.

Upstream of oblivion,
beyond the *here*,
home is the secret:
tomorrow, perhaps
once again, shall we know
how to enjoy it?

THE POEM WORMS

Each man is this Aleph
who in the *here*
wakes universal
oblivion, and makes
the simple life of the dead
world reappear.

LESSON OF THE SHOAH

Lo tirtsa'h

Out of the fire
our bare feet have carried us
a long time over the nocturnal earth:
among the withered brambles,
across a desert of stones
a desert of stars, where the years
of our life, one by one, fell,
ripe figs in the shadows.

And now as before
on this wasteland where we go our way
murder alone is held in honour:
in our gardens, in our houses,
terror's echo
always remains in season.

Fifty years after the Shoah
history awaits its new victim:
will we never have done with
the burden of such a life?
In the hell of his heart
the deep need to torture
of the man without Torah without love,
takes the place of paradise.

Inhabited
by his bad dream,
in the icy fire of anger

his faith is rekindled.
Every hangman turns
into the high priest of the abyss;
when all is said and done,
for Cain our brother
– Eve's favourite son –
the pleasure of killing remains
the one and only law.

IN THE EVENING...

In the evening when I listen to
Mozart's clarinet concerto,
the time of suffering, anxiety,
draws to an end, and suddenly
I am swimming in youth's golden light,
the shadow of old age is briefly rent,
our pliable bodies join together
in the torrent of our hair borne by the wind:
their joy illuminates the sky of love,
life's anguish has become as light as air.

THE DEAD ARE STUBBORN...

The dead are stubborn: their insistence they
live on scares me. When I recall my youth
my knotted throat swallows a dying tear,
this winter suddenly nostalgia flowers.

In the woods a footpath flees towards the sun,
my mother's laugh scurries beneath the branches:
but that day's died without leaving a trace,
among the dead leaves not one soul remains.

Oh where have you gone my dear lost shades?
In the thick of night, each one, alone, descends
the steps of the abyss towards his fate

into a place where none is seen again.
If you seek the embers you must plough the ashes
in the deep fire's core pulsating under snow.

SONG OF THE IMMIGRANTS

Braving night and cold,
hunger and wind,
scores of enemies:

see them tread through
the fields in search
of heaven on earth.

Two dogs from the heart
of Brittany:
Radish and Doe-skin,

seasoned warriors,
their narrow snouts
dotted with grey hair,

late in life heading
for Paris, a share
of happiness...

ANCIENT REMINGTON

My machine is fifty-four years old:
I was seventeen
when I bought it after the first *bac*
second hand in Strasbourg,
rue Finkmatt, at Uhl-Bonaventure's.

In Toulouse, Boston and Jerusalem
my faithful typewriter
has clicked away beneath my fingers
gently aging
with my poetry.

SUMMER PSALM

One evening among the evenings in time's orchard
which flowers, germinates, burns up and dies,
I filled my basket with laughter and with tears
to throw a great bridge over the day of sorrow
towards the sons and daughters of our
        grandchildren
perched in the apple tree sparkling with sap.
Dancer prince cradled by the morning wind
a living spring
will leap from earth's navel tomorrow
between the dream's turf and the thick dark mist.
There our fruits ripen
in the double light
of the late moon and the rising sun
that my summer psalm
promises in marriage to its night.

CENTAUR'S SUN

In the wind's laugh
whinnies the centaur's sun:
death is unknown,
life unfathomable!
For a long time
the black sky will turn blue
in the secret heart of heaven,
for a long time
the earth will flower in spring
over the dark sea.
But, still, man will expire
in this purple neighing:
bloody seed hurled
into the womb of space
like a bramble bush aflame with terrible stars –
when the quadruple hoof,
raised up in ecstasy,
of the horse rearing
as it cries into the night
strikes the rock
with its nails of steel.

ON A LATE INTERMEZZO OF BRAHMS

Bullfinch, cock-chafer, firefly,
when the melody is played
what remains of our life?

At the end as in the beginning
some faces without words,
madness and mourning will darken.

Bull-finch, cock-chafer, firefly,
as soon as the play is over,
will take wing on the breath of night:

Bull-finch, cock-chafer, firefly,
silence is our final melody.

A PHONECALL FROM NEW YORK

All our friends have left to dance
the night away
under the rainy earth.
Soon we shall be the only ones
turning in the night
among strangers who pass by
and do not see us
and do not speak to us
in human language.

Why do the dying burn
devoured by fever
if not to freeze tomorrow
in the grey dawn
in the winter mud?
And why must they cry
throughout the night,
to die in the morning
their hair matted in sweat?

Soon we shall wander
lost
among these strangers
with whom we had never danced,
nor laughed:
they would not have even
recognised our faces
in the improbable brightness
of original dawn.

Already our playmates have left us;
one by one, without saying a word,
they have signed up for winter
sports in the school of oblivion.
Bending in the December rain
the storm decks out with brief cold stars,
a single cypress tree
sparkles as it whirls
in the squally darkness.

PROSE

1.

My father is going on seventy, my mother a few
years younger. I'm already nearly half way.
There they are at the age of *their* parents when I
knew them and captured the latter's childhood
through my own in memories raised from the
depths of their old age. My children are begin-
ning to take their own place in the sun. Life is a
carnival procession in which the masks are
changed from generation to generation and from
age to age until the final one – earth's mask no one
can ever remove from us. Death reveals the iden-
tity which was hidden in us beneath so many
disguises: the mask of Nobody. We embody the
masks. Only the procession is real.
    Refuse to distinguish between your thought
and your direct vision of the things of the world,
between inner states and the treasures which
invade us by way of the senses. It is not a ques-
tion of sacrificing one to the other, but of remain-
ing faithful to the initial fact of human experience
represented by their simultaneous outpouring.
Spiritual intuitions and apprehensions of space
are indissociably linked. To betray this is to have
already falsified everything – reconstructed, sug-
gested, fabricated, re-presented, instead of wit-
nessing what has been taking place: our only real
task as poets.

....

Having attained a certain perfection in the quotidian austerity of life, one ends by seeking distraction only in what is essential: air, ice, birds, children, the deep oval lake of your belly, the tree of your nape, the white fire of the stars in the coal mine of the sky. All this remains, even here, part of the condition of deprivation, which is uprootedness. Thus for lack of worldly accidents or stimulants the very substance of the world will be the serious business of our life. As a subject of conversation it's limited. But what price this reduction to elemental clarity, to the all-powerful vital minimum of exile, of our lives formerly so demanding and greedy for wonders? In exchange for all the rest we have learned to be enchanted only by what is.

....

Poetic speech is the womb of time. It says always: "Here begins..." and the phrase remains unfinished, without subject or object. I shall not cease giving birth to my father!

....

The poetic act becomes possible when we are already stripped of requirements, having delivered ourselves to the shadows without laying

down any conditions – deprived of ourselves and
of the world. Form this premature little death
creation is accomplished. Then the reborn soul
can lay itself open, with delight, to the reborn
morning. The poem's joy rises in a sepulchre.
Out of silence speech leaps forth. Always know
how to hear it in this way.

....

Outside, the words of strangers reign for ever. I
have no one to speak to. I write these notes for
want of an interlocutor. I pursue this enforced
soliloquy to fill a lack, to exorcise a threatening
absence. Here I consign the relationships I could
not otherwise have: my waiting is shown in relief,
the hollow form of exile beyond words. Thus little
by little this journal becomes the aberrant summa-
tion of my silences, eye-witness of my night.

from *Journal de l'été indien* in *L'été indien*,
Gallimard, Paris 1957

2.

October 17 1947

A few days ago I bought Bach's Mass. After four
months of harassment and temporal worries –
doctoral thesis, house, money – listening to this
music has at last pointed me in my true direction,
from which the practical requirements of the hour
had succeeded in diverting me: my destiny is to be
a poet, nothing else. All the rest must be inte-
grated with this fundamental obligation: to create.
At last I am going to cease, after years of compro-
mise with things of second or third importance,
wasting my time by "employing" it to the detri-
ment of the act of creation. I feel within myself
great hidden reserves. Gone the worst epochs
when I had no choice but to sacrifice myself to
everyday nastiness, henceforth I want to conse-
crate myself, as fully as possible, to my true voca-
tion. I believe that in the last analysis this is the
unique destiny of an artist: if he betrays his art all
other "successes" are nothing but a bitter mock-
ery, for to realise those feats of valour there was
no special reason to be a poet. It was enough to
grind straight ahead. It is extremely difficult to
maintain an equilibrium between the demands
imposed by external contingencies, the work these
dictate, the stupid amount of time they gobble up
– and the creative mission, which alone counts
when all is said and done. That such an equilib-
rium is possible without having to renounce the

principal thing, some great names furnish the proof. Goethe and Bach for example. Then there is the heart-rending example of Beethoven. He shows that if anything has to be renounced, it is everything else. Unless a new war interferes before long, I think I have arranged my material situation solidly enough to find at last the indispensable calm and free time required for my projected work. What is unique in Bach is the vigour he put into his very life, simple and even humble as it was, but free and respected, out of which flowed that unparalleled work for which he lived, fought, taught solfeggio and Latin grammar for thirty years, without hoping for anything, enjoying neither the glory he merited, nor the affluence that spirits less noble but more business-like would have achieved by dint of compromise with life. In the rottenness of our time, as of his, the example of that man is the rallying point for those who – rare indeed – do not resign themselves to the facile and illusory successes of the quotidian. The Credo, the Sanctus, the Agnus Dei of Bach's great Mass, raise us to our level of virtual being, return us to the authentic homeland of the soul, from which the claws of routine tend ceaselessly to tear us despite our aspiration to join our true place.

....

ART POÉTIQUE

I survive among ruins. The meaning of the field of excavations does not lie in its surface, but in its depth: simultaneous upheaval of the places and times of completed experience, rising today in this syncopated rhythm, the only authentic one, which uncovers at one and the same time the ruptures – shards, fragments of bones or architecture, an original richness frittered away in obliterated coins – and the all-embracing totality underlying the discreet vestiges of a defunct society. Thus the poem... For the linear succession of finite moments, linked together in series, for the painted surfaces of the novel, substitute the polyhedral simultaneity of times and places felt by the senses: synchronous expansion of a sphere of lived experience with thousands of translucent facets refracting compact layers of discontinuous beings and events, that agglomerate as they totalise themselves freely for the first time in a gigantic ocular prism to capture, finally, the entire presence in the world of a man in transit through life! Forge the single eye of the Cyclops.

....

[T]he condition of the poet born in Alsace… What link can be established or restored between the moments of epiphany – divine or infernal – and their linguistic manifestation? What relationship between the language of the poem (the language of every day, if one wants a more appropriate word) and "the sweet native tongue" of the soul? What relationship between "a charlatan's transition" (Rousseau) and the joy or agony of expression? Maurice Blanchot, who has read my remarks on being an Alsatian poet, refers me to a text of Heidegger affirming that provincial dialects are "the secret source of every full-grown language". Through them would be redeemed "institutional signs" and that "old poetical stuff" which Rousseau was rightly suspicious of, as was Rimbaud later on. Would the survival, in a writer, of a "deictic" pre-language underlying the written word, of a patois at one with the brute density of things, deprived of "transitional" resources as well as of outmoded artistic conventions, permit the salvation of the formal poem today, or even of formal speech itself, which would emerge after many dangerous metamorphoses? This stream of thought leads me to defend, against terrorists and professional denigrators of accepted language, a certain realistic form – in the medieval sense of the term – for poetry and prose yet to be written. Rhetoric can be justified only on the basis of a non-rhetorical experience, lived by consciousness when confronted by the real, and faced with total dearth. My living eye before this broken piece of grey stone: that is a legitimate point of departure. The "charlatan's transition" is freely accepted only when linked to a primordial state of palpable existence plunging first of all into the very marrow of the given which has been so deeply felt. In Rousseau's eyes "developed acts" (wonderful formula for reasoning and analysis in opposition to intuitive visions) are of worth only through "the dumb admiration that the contemplation of the works" of visible Creation excites. Conversely, upon this overwhelming and unanswerable "admiration", upon the ecstasy of light where the simple and peaceable reign of Presence flourishes, a poetical rhetoric and discursive charlatanry can be based, without too much delusion in respect of reality. One must begin with human beings in order to end with words, and not reckon on the possibility of reaching into the substance of people, or even hinting at this, given the existence of words. In this operation which moves from the silence of things to the precise utterance in which that silence would reverberate, the mediating and salutary role of a patois seems self-evident. As does the damage wrought in the poetical function of the spirit by a too calculated and over-articulated language dedicated, like the academic French which is our inheritance, to the purest "charlatan's transition" between nothing and nothing, between word and word.

....

100

Only he who *is* can accept, smiling, that he will be no more. For death and the void are themselves prerogatives of being. The living dead fear death and miss out on the life they do not have. Orpheus envies and seeks elsewhere than in himself the being he is deprived of. He lives off nostalgia. He pursues the shade of Eurydice because seeking *himself* he does not possess himself. He who has being does not descend into hell to recover it. To have once possessed it is enough, sings Hölderlin gravely. He who has being accepts loss, with a strange smile, because he is already beyond all loss. *He exists entirely within death, here and now.* He who is nostalgic for plenitude, being deficient in his own being, cannot accept to die. He regrets, he weeps, therefore he does not exist. He would never consent to the loss of a being which he has not known how to incarnate within himself. But he who smiles in the face of death knows that being *is*, at the very heart of loss. For him nostalgia becomes useless. He is already transported in spirit beyond farewells. He has received his share of splendour in this world.

from *La Lune d'hiver*, Flammarion, Paris 1970

3.

Man aspires with all his senses, with all his inner
faculties, towards happiness and towards that
blossoming of his love which justice within the
imperishable dominion of reason prepares for
him. He responds to this call through the liberat-
ing forces of his history. At certain moments the
measured whirl of his language in the purest
fields of imaginary space yields a similar impulse.

In every shadowy or tormented period of col-
lective existence, which he shares with his brother,
with his rival, poetry presents him with a doubt-
less tragic vision of himself, but whole and
achieved, happy (let us say) because torn from the
incompletion which was continuing to disfigure
him.

Witnessing nobly to his real future, amid the
doubts and contradictions of his century, poetry
revives in him the heroic passion which bears him,
often unknowing, to redemption – ultimate and
impossible – on earth.

Confronting him suddenly with his virtual and
future face, the only original one, poetry leans on
him to bring about in this world, and at once, his
own transfiguration within the human order. Not
in the manner of Lucifer who supplants in order
to satisfy his particular pride and pleasure, but
like the disciple, always dearest to his heart, of his
secret master, of that Adam Kadmon – the first
man to share his secrets, and in whom at last he
recognised himself: son of ancient man. The one

of whom it was said in a dream: "Justice will surround his flanks; he will pronounce in the name of the law on behalf of the wretched of the earth". Only the immediate recalling of this destiny, this promise, this obligation, confers on poetry its spiritual bearing in this world, and guarantees its human dignity at all times. As long as it remains faithful, in this way, to its essential nature, poetry will not fail in its universal mission.

from *Délivrance du souffle*, Flammarion, Paris 1977

4.

(from an interview)

You are a writer. You have published essays, narra-tives, journals, poems but in the end you would choose to be described as a poet.

– Yes. Because narratives and essays constitute attempts at elaboration of the thematic cores of my poems. These throbbing cores are the primary elements of my sensibility. I am a storyteller but in no way a novelist. I am not gifted with the ability to invent characters or situations. But those that I live, those that I note around me, I seize them with my gaze, I garner them, I make them my own, and I know how to make them live in the eyes of others because I love to recount them. From mouth to ear first of all; in the secret of the thing written down, finally.

[................]

For the world in which we live to have a meaning, it must not be limited to words alone: let these not exist for their own sakes and let them therefore not be objects of idolatry; *it is essential that*, in the consciousness of each member of a human group, and among those who lead them, *the way words are used be a function bringing more life to bear on things.* If not, language is enclosed in a kind of speech machine which is no longer the organ responsible for the valorisation of life. Words can then be arbitrarily employed; they are reified in the verbal apparatus: their meaning is undermined, finally denied and obliterated. As Kafka said: "The true word leads, the false word misleads".

The peoples prey to this voluntary or passive confusion of languages are themselves soon devoured, swept along by it into universal war. For those who have not kept the primary consciousness of the Good active within themselves, words are condemned to freeze into deathmasks, or to undergo a diabolical reversal of meaning. Then utterance becomes a weapon of death, in a world of murder and suicide. Fo me that goes without saying, but it is neither self-evident nor easy to demonstrate to anyone who sets his face against it. Remember Mallarmé's claim: the world exists to end up in a beautiful book.

from *Le Parfum et la cendre*, Grasset, Paris 1984

5.

THE POET'S PLACE

At the very moment of the creative experience, consciousness recapitulates its entire being, whose incandescent multiplicity is revealed to it in one swoop – beyond the manifest images of the memorial past – by its total sense of existence. It brings about the capture of self-knowledge as such. This is not a random process. The elements consciousness draws towards its centre at that moment and which it keeps hold of later on, are not accidents in the immense series of events in the past or present. They correspond, as Proust writes, to significant markers staked out on the unique curve of the past which nourishes human consciousness, with its personal memories, its specific hallucinations. The reiteration of the total curve of experience is already inscribed, without any longer having to refer to objects determined by individual experience or imagination, in the global existential feeling of consciousness galvanised in depth. Whence the "pre-established harmony", vouched for by Proust, among the innumerable nuances of musical composition and in the synchronous existence relived in memory, and "a ground-swell which makes [the composer's] song eternal and immediately recognisable". It is in this groundswell that the true composer submerges and reconciles the multiplicity of his work: "he begins to sing that remarkable song whose monotony – for whatever the subject dealt with the song remains identical to itself – proves the fixity of the constituent elements of his soul. But then isn't it the case that these elements, all the residue of the real we are bound to keep for ourselves, [...] the ineffable which qualitatively differentiates what each of us has felt and is bound to abandon at the very threshold of phrases where he can communicate with others only by limiting himself to exterior particulars common to all and without interest, art [...] makes all of it visible, exteriorising through the colours of the spectrum the intimate composition of those worlds we call individuals and which without art we would never understand? This return to what was not to be analysed was so intoxicating, that on leaving this paradise my contact with more or less intelligent people seemed to me of extraordinary insignificance". (*La prisonnière*, "Le septuor de Vinteuil").

Normally, after childhood, the active self, with its established habits, the weight of its personal past – what Croce calls the empirical and voluntary personality – becomes an integral part of consciousness, to the point where they cannot be distinguished. Consciousness attaches itself to the empirical personality whose fate it shares and influences. This is why in adults, when the empirical self abdicates, consciousness generally weakens along with it; henceforth it no longer has any fulcrum in reality, completely merged with the radius of action of the practical self now abolished. Things can be described differently in the case of the creative artist. During the creative experience a divorce is temporarily established between the practical self, reduced to an ancillary state, and consciousness liberated from its companion in social thrall. Consciousness survives the "fall" of the empirical personality, and becomes more acute as a result of this very separation. It draws new strength from its own substance through a sort of involution, then contracts – from the very fact of this internal metamorphosis – a new alliance with phenomenal reality ("representations"). In this new relationship, old representations change their character because they are now being conjured up by a healed consciousness, renewed in its very strength and purity. It has rediscovered its authentic destination which directs it self-wards. Poetic vision takes the place of practical vision; synthetic perception – totalising and formal –, an absolute perception, takes the place of analytical perception, fragmentary and referring to social conventions. Abstract feeling, decanted from its milieu of original experience, makes way for a concrete sensibility still bathing in its unique existential situation shot through with an objective exaltation and linked from the very beginning with the latter's formal figuration. Inner and outer are but one reality, primitively experienced as such by the fired consciousness. The world starts anew, and poetry is born with it.

In this uncommon state of the consciousness which creates, words and their objects necessarily find a primeval identity: they coincide, because transformed consciousness again finds within itself the energy for the primary naming of things, which is the origin of language. This binding energy was engendered by originative consciousness at its very dawning. Then the erosion of vitality, the gradual weakening of spoiled thought, compelled to a marriage of reason with the practical personality, began to cause the progressive rupture of the unity of words and things. The power rediscovered by consciousness descending into itself permits a new welding with its objects. It effaces the depredations of empirical life without denying the truth of the latter, and recharges language by reuniting it simultaneously with things restored to their ontological dignity and the new consciousness of which language is the concrete reflection. According to Baudelaire, "the imaginative person says: 'I want to illuminate things with my mind and project the reflection onto other minds'". What reflection is he thinking of? That of things, or of his mind? At the moment of creation in action, this distinction can no longer be made; for Baudelaire, there is objective existence, concrete reality of "my mind" acting in substance – by means of reflection in things equally real and seized in words – on other minds who thus participate in the triple world of words, things and the mind of Baudelaire. The mind exists concretely, its action being a self-manifestation. The poem is the place of this action, where the beings of the world, the words of language and the creative spirit of man all merge.

This implies a conception of mental architecture, according to which consciousness could co-exist with itself at several levels, in various distinct and characterised states, determined by the real conjuncture of the lived moment: sleep, practical activity, deduction and abstract reasoning (scientific activity), or meditation of a creative nature. Creative activity and creative attitude would correspond to a specific level of consciousness, in the same way as other major forms of mental comportment. There would therefore exist a psychic distance more important than you might think between the true unconscious and the "normal" (practical and empirical) activity of consciousness. In this intermediate mental space is situated the creative activity of the artist. By involution, empirical consciousness takes up its abode there after a primary phase of the process of invention. Artistic activity is a type of behaviour realised in full consciousness – but carried out by means of a very special method of working. Artistic creation takes place neither at the level of abstract consciousness which characterises scientific thought, nor at the level of empirical or practical consciousness dominated by the active self, nor in the subsoil of the individual's unconscious, nor in the pre-historic bedrock of the latter as Jung's theses would have us believe. It is carried out in the very heart of consciousness modified by involution. Words, objects, images – archetypal phantasms included – crystallise as poem in the median constellation of the psychic sky. The unconscious does not create ex-nihilo, does not dispatch the poem ready made into consciousness which happens to be innocently overhanging. Unconscious material is arranged according to the lines of force emanating from consciousness modified by involution. It gives itself up to the latter which informs it in depth in accordance with its capacity of an affective, cognitive, formal order, finally recuperated and functioning in unison. Creative activity is a type of behaviour distinct from any other method of the productive workings of consciousness. The poet must hold onto this while not transgressing the limits of his real field of activity.

CLAUDE VIGÉE

Claude Vigée, born in Bischwiller (Lower Rhine) on 3 January 1921, comes from a Jewish family established in Alsace for more than three hundred years. His grandparents were drapers, and traders in grain, nuts and hops.

His childhood was spent in the marshy wooded region of the Ried on the shores of the Rhine. At the time his birthplace was still a centre of the textile industry which had been set up in the eighteenth century by Huguenot refugees after the revocation of the Edict of Nantes. In the years following the first world war the Alsatian dialect was mainly spoken.

In 1939, having completed his secondary studies at the classical college in Bischwiller and the Lycée Fustel de Coulanges in Strasbourg, he was evacuated and then expelled from Alsace with all his family when the Nazis occupied the area.

While studying medicine, he helped organise Jewish resistance in Toulouse – from October 1940 till the end of 1942 – against the Nazi occupiers and the Vichy government.

His first poems were published by Pierre Seghers at Villeneuve-lès-Avignon in the resistance magazine, *Poésie* 42. There he met Louis Aragon and Pierre Emmanuel, the latter his life-long friend.

Having reached the United States as a refugee at the beginning of 1943, he married his cousin Evelyne after the war and completed his doctorate in Romance languages and literatures in 1947.

He taught French literature at Ohio State University, Wellesley College and Brandeis University. From 1956 to 1959 he was Chairman of the Department of European Literature at Brandeis. His children Claudine and Daniel were born there in 1948 and 1953.

During this period he corresponded with T.S. Eliot and André Gide. He met Saint-Jean Perse, Jorge Guillen, Gaston Bachelard, Albert Camus, Paul Celan.

In 1950 his first book of poems, *La Lutte avec l'ange*, was published in Paris. In 1954 Pierre Seghers published his second book. In 1957 Albert Camus accepted *L'Été indien* for Gallimard. In 1962 *Le Poème du retour* was published by Mercure de France.

He and his family arrived in Israel in 1960. He became Professor of French and Comparative Literature at the Hebrew University in Jerusalem, where he taught till 1983. He was Chairman of the Department of Romance Studies from 1963 till 1967 and of Comparative Literature from 1970 till 1972. His friends included Martin Buber, Gershom Scholem and Leah Goldberg. Since retiring in 1984 he divides his time between France and Jerusalem, with visits to Germany, Italy and Greece.

Claude Vigée has received various prizes, including the Jacob-Burckhardt Prize (Switzerland, 1977), the Fémina-Vacaresco Prize for Criticism (Paris, 1979), the Johann-Peter Hebel Prize

(Germany, 1984) and the Grand Prix de Poésie of the Société des Gens de Lettres (Paris, 1987). There have been three colloquia on his work: Ben-Gurion University, Beer-Sheba 1985; Cérisy-la-Salle, 1988; Université des Sciences Humaines, Strasbourg 1989.

His translation of T.S. Eliot's *Four Quartets*, done nearly fifty years ago, has finally been published (The Menard Press in association with King's College, London 1992).

from *A CONVERSATION WITH CLAUDE VIGÉE*
BY FREEMA GOTTLIEB.

The Resistance gave Claude Vigée his first experience of
Jewishness as history in the making. Escaping to unoccu-
pied France in June 1940, he became a medical student in
Toulouse. There he met up with an international group of
young refugees, writers, musicians, artists, Zionist dreamers,
avid readers of the Prophets and the Psalms, fugitives from
all over Nazi-occupied Europe, each one often the sole
survivor of an entire family, an entire village, yet with the
high spirits to salvage from the Nazi cataclysm the dream of
the remaking of a people.

One night in May 1941 Vigée was blindfolded and led
through backstreets to the headquarters of the Jewish
Resistance in Toulouse, and sworn into a group calling itself
'The Strong Hand', from the Biblical verse, "For with a
strong hand shall I take you out... (from Egypt)." (Exod.
13:9). Only years later did he discover that the Resistance
cell containing the friends he met up with by seeming
chance in Toulouse, had all the time been masterminded by
the Irgun in far-off Palestine.

Vigée's mixed unit of religious and secular Zionists
centred on Ariadne, the beautiful daughter of the great
Russian composer Alexander Scriabin. Just at the time the
deportations were getting underway, she converted to
Judaism to marry a non-religious Jew, herself becoming
deeply religious. (She was publicly gunned down by the
French militia in Toulouse in 1944.) Even in times of great
danger, these young friends wrote poetry, discussed ideas,
and arranged lectures on synagogue art even as the great
European synagogues were being destroyed.

Since his family had lived in French Alsace for at least ten
generations, going back to Louis XIV, unlike "foreigners"
like Ariadne and her husband, Vigée had the right even
under Vichy to come and go as a free person. He used this
to full advantage by acting as a link between the Resistance
and the network of Jewish centres in the South, from the

Pyrenees as far as the Rhône valley, in a zone that included Toulouse, Pau, Lyon, Marseille, and Nice. His job was to recruit new members for the Resistance, and also to transmit information.

When warned by Resistance comrades that his name had been blacklisted, he and his mother were lucky enough to obtain doctored exit papers to travel across the border to Spain, and then on to Portugal, from where Vigée managed finally to get to the United States. There he first tasted true exile which, together with the longing for "origins", was to be the driving force of his writing. For Vigée, love of family, of native land, of one's personal landscape or origins are essential and legitimate thirsts of any one who is truly alive. All this he felt himself deprived of when he came to live in the United States.

Even though Vigée was reunited in America with Evelyne, his cousin and childhood sweetheart of the first summer of the war, his writings from that period do not convey a sense of personal happiness. As a young French poet he felt his whole future to be meaningless in a culture that did not speak to him in his own language. He thought it was crazy to bring children into a world where he felt he had virtually nothing in common with this neighbours.

On arrival, he worked at a whole range of menial jobs while studying for a doctorate in literature at Ohio State Univeristy. The wrench from Europe brought about by Hitler's genocide forced him to speak English, teaching him the "relativity of languages and peoples". Later he taught French and Comparative Literature at Wellesley College and eventually chaired the French Department at Brandeis University. In retrospect, he could understand that the seventeen years he spent in the United States served the positive function of enabling a clean break with his beloved France (which, in effect, by passing the "Jewish Statute" stripping its Jews of their human rights and native citizen-ship, had opportunistically betrayed them) and of preparing him for the country of his even more atavistic origins and of his still uncertain future, Israel.

In a sense, Vigée's whole œuvre amounts to a yearning for lost origins, a perennial nostalgia transcended through return to Jerusalem, the "origin of origins." And yet, there remains the ache of betrayal that he tried to overcome. As he himself writes: "Our true source is not among existing things."

Physical return to Jerusalem was accompanied (he felt) by an inner movement of reintegration with ancient roots. Vigée sees in the exile of the "Peuple-Christ" nothing less than a crucifixion on the Tree of History. The Messianic people in one way or another is martyred by the nations. Yet, "with us, exile is always close to joy".

Exile is perhaps the central theme in all Vigée's writing, the creative interplay, for example, between Israel and Diaspora. But is also involves a refusal of the physical world and an artificial relationship with language. While in 2,000 years of exile Jewish poets have been deprived of a natural relationship with language and with things, now that Israel exists Jewish writers, even in the Diaspora, can use language naturally. Essentially their capacity to sing has been restored to them!

His poems proclaim a faith in a fragile "Living word", in a God sometimes manifest in light and water and earth of nature and the Holy Land, and rooted in the dark centre of all human lives. The person I met in his austere apartment in the Rue des Marronniers, was a man partly vindicated by history. Both he and the "Children of Israel" had temporarily come through. His return to Israel made sense of his Resistance experiences in France, his alienation as a French poet in the United States.

BOOKS BY CLAUDE VIGÉE

L'Été indien (poèmes et journal de *L'Été indien*),
    Gallimard, 1957
Les Artistes de la faim (essais critiques), Calmann-Lévy, 1960
Révolte et Louanges (essais critiques), José Corti, 1962
Moisson de Canaan, Flammarion, 1967
La Lune d'hiver, Flammarion, 1970
Le Soleil sous la mer (poèmes 1939-1971), Flammarion, 1972
Délivrance du souffle, Flammarion, 1977
Du bec à l'oreille (album de textes), Éd. de la Nuée-Bleue,
    Strasbourg, 1977
Claude Vigée, par Jean-Yves Lartichaux, coll. « Poètes
    d'aujourd'hui », Seghers, 1978
L'Art et le Démonique (essais), Flammarion, 1978
L'Extase et l'Errance (essai), Grasset, 1982
Pâque de la parole, Flammarion, 1983
Le Parfum et la Cendre (entretiens), Grasset, 1984
Les Orties noires (poèmes et prose), Flammarion, 1984
Heimat des Hauches, Elster, Baden-Baden, RFA, 1985
Une voix dans le défilé, Nouvelle Cité, 1985
La Manne et la Rosée (essai), Desclée de Brouwer, 1986
La Faille du regard (essais et entretiens), Flammarion, 1987
Wénderôwefir, Association Jean-Baptiste Weckerlin,
    Strasbourg, 1988
La manna e la rugiada, Ed. Borla, Rome, 1988
Aux sources de la littérature moderne I (essais),
    Entailles-Nadal, 1989
Le Feu d'une nuit d'hiver (poèmes), Flammarion, 1989
Leben in Jerusalem, Elster Verlag, Baden-Baden, 1990
Lire Claude Vigée, C.R.D.P., Académie de Strasbourg, 1990
Apprendre la nuit (poèmes et proses), Arfuyen, 1991
Dans le silence de l'Aleph (essais, 1986-1990),
    Albin-Michel, 1992
La Terre et le Souffle, Claude Vigée, Actes du colloque de
    Cerisy 1988, Albin-Michel 1992
Passage du Vivant (choix de poèmes et de proses), forthcoming

TRANSLATIONS BY CLAUDE VIGÉE

Cinquante poèmes de R. M. Rilke, « Les Lettres », 1953, et «
Jeunes amis du livre », 1957
Mon printemps viendra, poèmes de D. Seter, Seghers, 1965
Les Yeux dans le rocher, poèmes de David Rokéah, traduits de
l'hébreu, José Corti, 1968
L'Herbe du songe, poèmes d'Yvan Goll, traduits de
l'allemand, Editions Caractères, 1971; Arfuyen, 1988
Le Vent du retour, poèmes de R. M. Rilke, Arfuyen, 1989
Quatre Quatuors de T.S. Eliot, The Menard Press
(in association with King's College), 1992

NOTE ON THE TRANSLATOR

Anthony Rudolf was born in London in 1942. He has
written, translated or edited various books of poetry and
prose including, most recently, a trilogy of short texts of his
own:
At an Uncertain Hour: Primo Levi's War against Oblivion,
Menard 1990
Wine from Two Glasses: the 1990 Adam Lecture,
King's College 1991
I'm not even a grown-up: the diary of Jerzy Feliks Urman,
Menard/King's 1991
His translations include books by French and Russian poets:
Tvardovsky, Vinokourov, Bonnefoy and Jabès, as well as
Balzac's *The Unknown Masterpiece*. A selection of his own
poems, *The Same River Twice*, was published by Carcanet
Press in 1976 and another selection, *After the Dream*, was
published by Cauldron Press, St Louis, in 1979.